I0170046

THE IMPOSTER AUTHOR

Banish Author Imposter Syndrome

E Whelly

CSG Publishing House

Copyright © 2024 E Whelly

All rights reserved

The characters and events portrayed in this book are
fictitious. Any similarity to real persons, living or dead, is
coincidental and not intended by the author.

No part of this book may be reproduced, or stored in a
retrieval system, or transmitted in any form or by any
means, electronic, mechanical, photocopying, recording,
or otherwise, without express written permission of the
publisher.

ISBN-13: 978-1-7388536-5-6 ebook
ISBN-13: 978-1-7388536-6-3 paperback

Cover design by: Get Covers
Editing by : Erika Russell

This is for all the authors, writers, poets, collaborators and editors who thought they weren't good enough.

You are!

CONTENTS

CHAPTER 1

Introduction

Hi, my name is Em Whelly, and I am an author who has suffered from imposter syndrome. An imposter syndrome author, as I like to call it. You may be asking yourself, what is an imposter syndrome author? Well, that is what I am here to tell you.

An imposter syndrome author is someone who has published a book or is attempting to publish a book and feels like a fraud. I have published four books to date, been on the bestsellers list, won awards and received praise for my work, signed books, and been invited to big events where people came just to see me, yet I feel like a fraud. There's that little voice in my head that tells me I'm not good enough and that I'm wasting my time.

I know I am not the only one who feels this way, and this book is for those who suffer alongside me.

I don't have proof, but you'll never be able to convince me that every author doesn't experience this, whether they're a fledgling or one of the greats. It affects us all. It even causes some authors to release work under pseudonyms just to see if their work is successful without their experienced name. I've done this, and it was not the success I was looking for. I found myself publishing a book under an unknown name that was nowhere near my best work, and people were unwilling to trust it. So from now on, I release under the same name and make sure to publish to the best of my ability.

Imposter syndrome is not unique to authors; all professions can experience this, but I'll focus on myself and my fellow authors in this book.

Being in the publishing industry, I've met many authors, and some have become very close friends (I'll name-drop later). One of the most common topics authors talk about together is imposter syndrome. I've been to a writing retreat where I've had a crying session while drinking— I shit you not—Writer's Tears whiskey. Please note that this is not sponsored in any way by Writer's Tears, but if anyone from the distillery wants to have their people contact my people…please do.

Shove thirty authors into a room for an entire weekend, and imposter syndrome is bound to come up, just as it did at the retreat I attended. To my knowledge or memory (remember the whiskey mentioned above), there was not one person in the room who had not experienced imposter syndrome at some point in their career—and some even that night, me being one of them.

Now, one thing I will say is that when you have a friend who is an author who finds success in their work, you are absolutely supportive, proud, and happy to see them achieve their well-deserved praise, but alone in your room or in front of a blank page with a blinking cursor, that weighs on you. Questions run through your head, like why am I not getting the success they are? Why am I not still number one on the bestseller charts on Amazon? Why don't I have as many reviews? Why don't I have as many sales? (Side note here: do not share sales numbers with any other author for your mental health and theirs. More on this later.)

We constantly ask ourselves these questions. Why am I not doing more? Is it my writing? Are there holes in my story? Are my characters likable? It all boils down to one question: is my book good? I am here to tell you that no matter who you are as an author, myself included, your last book is never your best book. Your next book is.

After I published my first novel, I constantly compared myself to other authors and weighed my successes. This was one of the worst things I could've done. Once I started comparing myself to my friends in the industry, it chopped my ego down, put it through a meat grinder, and set it on fire. It took me a long time to get over it, and to be honest, I am still working every day to fight it off.

So, how did I shift my mindset and stop comparing myself to others? Well, I compared myself to myself. My biggest competition is now my last book. If I am not writing at a higher quality or creating a story that is better crafted than my last, I am not doing myself justice. My debut novel, *My Beautiful Ghosts,* achieved great success for being written by an unknown author. I hit number one on Amazon the day it was released, and I've sold a lot of books, but there's always someone out there selling more.

The new rule I've given myself, and my recommendation to others, is not to ask about or share sales numbers. It is not going to help your mental health or the mental health of other authors.

At the time, I felt amazing with the release of my book. I was on cloud nine, just like any author should be on the day of their first book release.

When the sales page on Amazon updated and I had that orange bestseller flag, I took a screenshot, cried, and sent it to my editor, Cary Caffrey. Yes, that's the first name-drop. For as long as I live, I will never forget what he said to me: "Now stop looking at your sales and start writing!"

At the time, I laughed it off, thinking it was a joke. It was written over social media, so I didn't realize I'd missed the meaning. The true message was to get working on the next one because this will fade, and it will fade fast.

In the last decade, self-publishing, or indie publishing, has taken the publishing world by storm, and rightfully so. For far too long, the publishing world has been ruled by the powers that be and have decided who is worthy and who is not. It all comes down to marketing. I've read countless books over the years, and there have, of course, been great books, good books, okay books, and just bad books. Of all the books I've read, some of my favorites are from self-published or indie-published authors. Just because something is traditionally published does not mean it is a good book. The same goes for self-published books. Just because it's a self-published book does not mean it's a bad book.

For many years, it was believed that self-published books were lesser because they were not *selected* by traditional publishers, but that is not true. I've read absolutely amazing books by self-published authors who have gone through the normal publishing process. They find editors for developmental editing, copyediting, and proofreading, just like any other author. They use designers for their covers and have those books formatted to perfection for printing and reading. They just cut out the middleman of a traditional publishing house and go right to a distributor.

I want to make one thing clear: I am not trashing traditional publishing houses or authors who have been traditionally published. I have many friends who are part of that world, and they do amazing things, but traditional publishing is not for everyone, and that's okay.

I own CSG Publishing House, where I

currently publish my own work and that of two other authors. For me, this was always going to be the path. I've had some of my work accepted by traditional publishers, but I ultimately decided it wasn't for me.

One thing to understand about me is that I am very ambitious, and I like to control situations. I was not okay with a publisher dictating what I wrote, picking my covers, deciding which direction I would go for stories, etc. The other big factor was that I was not going to give up large percentages of my sales to publishers when I could do the work myself. To be clear, I don't edit my own work or design my own covers. I hire out for that. I put up my own money to contract work so I can keep that percentage of my sales and control what happens to my work.

Some authors don't want to be a part of that process or want the responsibility of doing everything themselves, and that's why they go to traditional publishers. That's perfectly okay, too.

Whatever path you choose, it's your path, and it makes you no less of an author. Hell, you wrote a book. That shit is hard. Every time I finish a first draft, I cry. Not little tears of joy; I full-on bawl my eyes out the entire night. I have so much of my mental health wrapped up in everything I write because I can't write without voice and emotion. I feel everything. I'm an incredibly emotional person. It may not seem that way if you meet me in person. I've been known to come off as cold and bitter, but that is the exterior. It's not one I've chosen intentionally, either. I can't help that I have a resting bitch face. My lips naturally turn downward, and I absolutely refuse to get plastic surgery to repair it.

I'd contemplated getting plastic surgery many times to fix my downturned lips or my nose. I did have a rhinoplasty and septoplasty in 2022, but that was to repair a crushed nasal cavity from an injury I had when I was eight years old that I didn't realize impacted my breathing. When they repaired it, they straightened it out but left my nose looking as if it had never been broken in the first place.

Long story, but I tripped over a dog leash and fell face-first into a tree stump. That should tell you everything you need to know about my coordination.

Back to my emotions and my bitchy face. I can't and won't fix it because I've come to learn that this is my face, and I have to own that. This realization came in 2018 when I gave birth to my son. He looks identical to my husband except for his eyes. Those, he got from me. Thankfully. My eyes are the one thing I've always been complimented on. It grew to annoy me when people mentioned the deep dark blue color or how big they were, but now that I see them on my son, I have a new appreciation for them.

My son is why I won't get plastic surgery. Why would I change my face and look less like him? He's got my eyes, yes, and he looks like my husband, but if I change anything else about my face, I'm losing what genetic appearance I gave my son.

Back to the point of this. I look like a cold bitch, but I'm anything but on the inside. I have feelings, and those feelings are big. I can recall almost any interaction with any person I've spoken to. I won't always remember faces or names, but I will remember their words, and I will analyze those words over and over. I've had countless sleepless nights where I spent the entire night thinking about a conversation and whether there was a meaning I missed or if I should've said something different.

I am not good at speaking, but I can write. Apart from my imposter syndrome as an author, I also have ADHD (attention-deficit/hyperactivity disorder), and writing my thoughts down is the one way I can properly express them.

If you've spoken to me in person or on the phone, you may or may not have noticed that I sometimes mispronounce words, speak so quickly my words get jumbled, or completely lose track of what I was trying to say in the first place. That's because of my ADHD. My mind is always in overdrive, and my mouth cannot keep up with the words my brain is sending, but...my hands can. For me, writing is an escape from my ADHD because I can type or write out my thoughts fast enough that they come out how I intend them.

That is why I am an author. I have this crazy brain that creates all these stories, and I have to tell them to other people. If you ask me what my books are about, I will tell you that I have no idea what to say because it took me an entire book to tell the story. Then, I will rattle off a little blurb about my books that I had to write down and memorize because my mouth cannot process the avalanche of words that my brain creates in wanting to tell people about my books.

So, now that you've gotten to know me a little bit as both a person and an author, let's dive into imposter syndrome.

CHAPTER 2

I'm Invalidated by
My Own Doing

Imposter syndrome. When does it start? For some, it can start from the moment they decide to write a book; for others, it can come later. But when does it end? In my experience and from conversations with other authors...

Never.

Don't leave! Keep reading. I know I just dropped a huge bombshell on you, but stick with me on this.

Imposter syndrome has almost become a rite of passage for authors. If you have to ask yourself if you are an author after you've published a book, then you are an author. If you write, you are a writer.

This may be a controversial topic for some, but I want to preface by saying this is something I only apply to myself. The controversy is the difference between a writer and an author. I called myself a writer the moment I started writing, but I wouldn't call myself an author until my book was published. It was validation for me because of the start of my own imposter syndrome, but I am here to tell you that if you write and have to ask yourself the question, you absolutely are an author.

Looking back now, I definitely had imposter syndrome before I published my first book, but I didn't know it had a name at the time. I was like anyone else trying something new. I didn't feel like I belonged because I hadn't yet achieved anything, but achievement can mean something very different to any person you ask. As I mentioned before, my competition is not other authors; it's my last book. That's not me saying I am above other authors. That's me saying that I am my own worst enemy and in a never-ending battle with myself.

I haven't yet figured out whether this is a good thing or a bad thing, but I know it's definitely been hard on my mental health in terms of sales. As I mentioned in the last chapter, my debut novel had an amazing release, so when it came time for my new book, *The Rise of Vardya,* to be published, I had extremely high expectations.

In terms of quality, *The Rise of Vardya* is far superior to *My Beautiful Ghosts.* The story makes sense, the writing is of a much higher quality, the characters have more depth, and the world-building is on a completely different level. Still, it did not do as well as *My Beautiful Ghosts.* Even today, its sales have not passed those of my debut novel.

From here on out, I will refer to *My Beautiful Ghosts* as MBG and *The Rise of Vardya* as RoV.

The biggest difference between the two books, apart from the quality, is that they are completely different genres! MBG is a literary fiction novel about a dogsled racer who gets into a terrible accident and suffers from mental health issues as she navigates her recovery from the grief of losing her dogs because of a foolish decision she made. RoV is a fantasy/science fiction novel about a struggle for power in the world of Vardya told from six points of view. It's kind of like *Game of Thrones* in that they are morally gray characters who make decisions that either serve themselves or their beliefs.

My point is that they are completely different genres of books that have no business competing with each other.

MBG got to the number one spot on Amazon in its genre, and it took me a long time to come to terms with the fact that it was *not* in competition with RoV and vice versa. Despite everything I've said about how my biggest competition was my previous book, it isn't, but at the same time, it is. I've had to reconsider my definition of the competition of my books. In terms of writing quality, yes, my last book is my competition, but in terms of sales, I cannot put the two in the same weight class.

Literary fiction and fantasy go together like oil and water. While I love both genres, they have no business being in the same room together. I've had many people ask me about my decision to write multiple genres and use the same author name. I never understood why until I came to this realization.

I still refuse to separate my name for my books, regardless of what genre I write. I write exactly how I read books. I'm a mood reader. I can switch from a true crime and read fantasy right afterward or switch to a romance to a non-fiction about writing and then to a Christmas romance. I write the same way. To date, published or unpublished, I've written fantasy, literary fiction, supernatural, YA, non-fiction, poetry, short stories, etc. All different genres, but one thing in common, and that one thing is me. So, in light of that, I will continue to use E Whelly as my author name.

Back to why I shouldn't have compared the sales of MBG and RoV. Literary fiction and fantasy have vastly different readers. Literary fiction is also an extremely broad genre that sometimes—well, mostly—just feels like a big stamp that says, "This is fiction, but I don't know where the fuck to put this book." Fantasy is simple to identify. Most of the time, it's a made-up world with magic, dragons, and a wild adventure.

Fantasy is also an extremely hard genre to break into. The majority of the time, fantasy books have sequels and require you to have a following to keep the reader engaged throughout however many books you plan on writing to tell the story. RoV is a planned three-book story, while MBG is a stand-alone book.

Readers know that if they read MBG, they will get the end result at the end of the book. With RoV, readers have to put their faith in me that I will complete all three books and not leave them hanging if I fail. With each book, readers will look at it and judge whether they want to invest in you as an author by buying your first, then second, then third, and so on in that series. This was one thing I did not take into consideration when I published RoV.

Anyone will tell you that the more books you write, the more books you will sell, and they are right, but what they don't tell you is that if you switch genres, you are essentially starting at square one all over again in a different genre. Which is what I am doing yet again by writing this book instead of working on *The Secrets of Austerland*, which is the sequel to RoV.

One of the reasons I decided to write this book is because of my own imposter syndrome. I really start to feel my imposter syndrome roughly three months after the launch of a new book. I get to the point where I see some sales come in, and it feels good at the moment, but then... It's like you have an addiction, and you go through withdrawal, needing the rush of publishing another book. You are always chasing the high of having your book in the spotlight, but then another book by another author comes along and dethrones you from that number one spot, and you are right back to feeling invalid.

I only feel validated as an author one month before launch until the dethroning of my book, when no one is interested in talking about it anymore. I've found that going through this book launch withdrawal leads to my imposter syndrome, bringing me to the dreaded writer's block.

CHAPTER 3

Writer-Induced Writer's Block

The hilarity of writer's block is that we never don't know what we should be writing; it's that we don't know how to write it. I don't know a single author who doesn't have a drawer of half-written manuscripts, ideas logged in a secret journal, or multiple projects on the go when they get burned out on another. In my opinion, it is not a lack of creativity; it's a lack of self-understanding and imposter syndrome that keeps us from writing.

I asked an author friend once how to get past writer's block, and he told me to ask myself what needs to happen in the scene I'm working on and write it. Even if it is one sentence that says, "Character A has a miscommunication with Character B, and they argue." That is progress. You wrote that scene. Now, all you have to do is fill in the gaps.

I've used this method many times when I've struggled writing a scene or chapter, and I have found great success, but what about when I can't physically write the words because I am terrified that I am not skilled enough or don't believe I am the author to write that scene? That's how my imposter syndrome steps into the room. My brain starts firing off negative affirmations about how MBG was all luck and the RoV series will never be finished because I'm a starter, not a finisher.

It hurts when someone else says these things to you, but it's worse when you think these things about yourself. I'm my biggest enemy, and no one can hurt me like I can.

I am my worst critic. Like any author, I have had one- and two-star reviews where people say they don't like my book or characters, and that doesn't faze me a single bit. Honestly, I don't care if you don't like my books. If someone bought one of my books, read it, and gave it a one-star review, all I have to say to that person is...nothing. They read my book, bought it, rated it, and moved on. I won because they bought and read my book.

Reviews are not for authors; they are for other readers. I've gotten new readers because of bad reviews, and I have seen other people purposely look for bad reviews and read based on that. What someone may not like, someone else undoubtedly loves.

There is not one single book on earth that is unanimously loved, and there never will be. It could be extremely well written with amazing characters, but there are people out there who will hate it. And that's okay.

When I see a low rating on one of my books, I look at it as a win. I reached someone outside my book's genre, and they still read it. It may not be for them, but they took the time to read the book in the first place, and they reviewed it.

So many authors get their underwear twisted about bad reviews, but do you honestly want to know what is worse? No review at all. If someone reads my book and doesn't leave a review, that's when I look at it as a loss.

That means I didn't spark enough emotion in that person, good or bad, for them to take one minute of their time to think about how they felt about the book once they reached that last page.

Also, word of advice to all authors reading this: NEVER RESPOND TO REVIEWS! Good or bad! Do not engage readers on their reviews of your books. I've witnessed situations where a reader left a bad review and the author responded negatively on both public and private platforms. This is highly unprofessional. Do as I said above. Take the win that they read and reviewed your book and move on.

I've seen situations where an author had their fan base stalk and harass a reviewer. That is absolutely not okay and should never happen! Readers should feel safe to share their reviews and thoughts on books, good or bad. Take it from the old saying, "No press is bad press."

Oscar Wilde once said, "There's only one thing in the world worse than being talked about, and that is not being talked about."

So, next time you see a bad review...smile and move on.

My own induced writer's block comes from the invalidation of my imposter syndrome, as has been mentioned many times throughout this book and will continue to be mentioned until the end.

Hi, my name is Em, and I am an author who has imposter syndrome because I let myself have imposter syndrome. Again, this stems from my insecurities as a person, which I never talk about out loud but am sharing with you all now. I am a highly insecure person, not because other people have invalidated me, but because I have invalidated myself.

Hi, my name is Em, and I'm the problem.

Cue Taylor Swift's "Anti-Hero."

I think no matter who you are, we all have a little bit of mental illness. I don't even think mental illness is truly an illness. It's a little extra flavoring that adds to our genetic makeup, and I think each person deals with it to a varying degree. I have ADHD and generalized anxiety disorder. They're part of me, and I've had to learn to navigate my life with them. Not everyone has these illnesses to the same degree.

I know some people who get nervous and get red splotches all over them when speaking in public. I know some people who have severe anxiety and can't leave their house without days of mental preparation.

With my anxiety and being an author, I get nervous around people I don't know and struggle with how to interact because I'm constantly trying to collect my thoughts and put together an intelligent sentence to add to the conversation without looking like a weirdo. This leads back to my ADHD and my brain not being able to send my mouth the words to say; sometimes there's a delay in my response or I trip over my words. Sometimes while I am trying to string these words together, I blank out and get that resting bitch face look, not because I'm mad or upset, but because I am trying to focus. It takes so much energy to say what I need to say that my face gives up and sends its efforts elsewhere.

This makes book events especially difficult for me because of my anxiety and ADHD. When I have a book signing, I spend the morning getting ready by not just taking a shower, putting makeup on, and collecting my books and marketing materials but mentally preparing myself to speak to strangers for an entire day and forcing a smile to stay on my face the whole time.

I listen to a specific playlist in my car every time I am on the way to a book event. Before I leave the car, I am either listening to Queen's "Don't Stop Me Now" or singing it in my head. It's my go-to get-pumped song.

After a book signing, I'm exhausted. My face

hurts from the forced smiling, and my brain is fried from the constant forced socializing. Don't get me wrong, I love book events, and I am extremely grateful to anyone who comes to see me, buys my book, and talks to me at an event, but it's not without a lot of effort on my part.

Because of the toll of book signings on my mental health, I do a limited amount of events per year and never close together.

I had one signing that lasted three hours, but I sold almost thirty books, and it was a constant lineup of people the entire time, whether they bought my book or just stopped by to say hi. Some have even previously bought my book and showed up just to have it signed. Like I said, I'm grateful, but after that event, I drove home in silence and took a four-hour nap.

My husband is very familiar with my author signing routine at this point and makes sure he takes care of our son, pets, and the house while I go through my wind-down process after an event.

I have a huge piece of advice for anyone doing a book signing. At every event I have been hired to do, they usually have a table for your books and a chair for you to sit on. Here's where the advice comes in: never sit in the chair. You stand the entire time, and you make eye contact, smile, and say hi to every person who comes into your line of sight. Trust me, they will stop and talk to you.

Another thing that I find extremely beneficial is asking people what kind of books they like to read.

I write multiple genres, so I can typically provide a genre they like. Plus, it gives you the chance to make the conversation about them. You aren't trying to force-feed strangers your books; you are asking them about themselves and trying to make a connection. Trust me. It works.

After the countless events I have attended, I've always done this, and I can guarantee you I have sold more books than other authors who attended book fairs the same day as me. I painfully watched a man across the aisle from me sit behind his table, which was decorated beautifully, but he didn't engage those walking by and looked scared to talk. He didn't sell a single book that day, and my heart ached for him.

Because I put so much effort into being an extrovert during my signings, it's very taxing on my social battery, and I've tried to find ways to make my recovery easier.

In the past year, I have found a new way to get through author signings with less stress, something I have come to rely on as of late, and that is going with another author.

My author bestie is Vanessa C. Hawkins. Vanessa and I have been doing events together for the past year. I love doing events with her. She is so outgoing and chatty that it takes the pressure off me so I have a chance to breathe and take a moment to myself between readers.

Aside from using Vanessa as my crutch, I truly enjoy our friendship and love spending time with her. We've had some great times at events and are always ready to step in and vouch for each other's books when we see a sale slipping.

Vanessa and I met at a book event, of course. We were both hired to do readings for the University of New Brunswick's Lorenzo Society. It was the first time I'd met her in person, but I'd been aware of her presence in the author community.

I totally fangirled over her when we met. I had a copy of her book, *Ballroom Riot,* which I made her sign for me after the event. I really wanted her to like me since I looked up to her in many ways. She is an established traditionally published author with a following and does not stick to one genre.

After the event, we added each other on social media and chatted on and off for the next little while until she asked me out for coffee. We went to this little coffee shop and ate cake as we sipped our hot drinks while chatting about our journeys to becoming authors. I will never forget the moment during that coffee date when Vanessa looked over my shoulder and saw a mouse running along the floor about ten feet behind me.

We were the only patrons in the spot. We should've known from the empty restaurant but had decided to give it a go regardless. Instead of getting mad about the little intruder, we both laughed, pushed aside our cakes, and finished our coffees.

We told the waitress, pointed out the mouse, which was not afraid at all, and watched the pure horror on this poor woman's face. That didn't stop us from laughing as she chased the mouse around the tables with a broom. Despite the unwelcome visitor, the waitress still got her well-deserved tip. It's not her fault Saint John is built on a swamp.

From that moment, Vanessa and I stayed in touch and decided to do our first event together. We had so much fun despite not selling many books at a used bookstore in Uptown Saint John. Still, it was my first step toward really building my friendship with her, and I will always cherish these memories.

I've leaned on Vanessa a lot when it comes to my imposter syndrome. She's always been there to be my hype girl, and I will forever love her for her unwavering support of me and my work.

CHAPTER 4

Banish It

Vanessa has talked me off the ledge many times. There have been days when I was ready to throw in the towel and say I was done writing books, but I've always found people to talk me out of it. Before this moment, the only people who had heard or read those words were my husband and other authors. I told my husband because he's my husband and we tell each other everything, but he doesn't truly get it, so that's why I turn to other authors.

Aside from Vanessa, there are other authors I have leaned on for support. Brandon J. Leblanc was my very first author friend. Brandon and I met in Cary Caffrey's novel writing group over Zoom in 2020 (third name-drop).

At the time, we were both unpublished authors, me working on MBG and Brandon working on *Exiles.* I think there was probably a good year and a half to two years that we talked to each other every single day. I shit you not. Every. Single. Day.

Brandon and I would send each other draft after draft, reading every word each other wrote, giving pep talks, pushing each other to write on days we didn't feel like it, and being an ear to vent to when needed. We started a tradition of sharing a drink of Writer's Tears whiskey and toasting each other's success each time we published a book.

Every time Brandon would make headway on his book, I worked harder to finish MBG, and vice versa. We were adamant that we were going to publish our work and weren't going to stop. We shared our first drink of Writer's Tears after I published MBG in June 2021 and again in February 2022 when he published *Exiles.*

I've found having author friends like Vanessa and Brandon to go through the writing process with is extremely helpful and validating. Both Vanessa and Brandon have experienced their own imposter syndromes, and it validated my own feelings.

It gave me proof that I am not the only one who feels this way. From Vanessa, who is a traditionally published author, to Brandon, who walked next to me through the process of publishing our first books. We all suffer from imposter syndrome.

Cary Caffrey once told me that if you worry about your work, want to make your next book better, or have days you feel like quitting, it just means you're an author. He said you are supposed to feel this way as an author. It gave me a lightbulb moment that set the rest of my feelings on imposter syndrome in motion.

If you're an author, you should expect to have imposter syndrome, whether that means having quick moments of wanting to give up or, like me, six months of self-loathing and not writing. Don't do that, though.

Instead of giving in to imposter syndrome, accept it for what it is and tell it to fuck off. Sorry if you think that's a bit crude. Feel free to change it to a more appropriate word, but banish the control imposter syndrome has over you and tell it to move on.

Find your support system and, maybe most importantly, go look at your author profile and list of published work. YOU ARE A FUCKING AUTHOR! You wrote and published work! Own that shit!

I am going to keep this book short and sweet for the sole purpose of helping you—yes, you— reading this. Get off your couch or out of bed, wherever you are, and sit down and write the damn book.

Go back and read this as many times as you need, but I want all you authors to say it with me right now. I will, too.

Okay, ready? Out loud now. On the count of three.

One... Two... Three...

I'm an author!

We said it! My husband just laughed at me and asked if I was giving myself positive self-affirmations.

You're damn right I am!

And you should, too.

Thank you for reading!

Thank you for reading this very short but necessary book on imposter syndrome in authors.

If you're not an author, thank you for your support.

If you are an author, go write the damn book and drink your celebratory Writer's Tears when you publish!

Oh! And don't forget to leave a review on Amazon and/or Goodreads. ;)

ABOUT THE AUTHOR

E Whelly

E Whelly was born in Saint John, New Brunswick. She's always had a strong love for books and creating stories. She is an avid coffee drinker and lover of whisky.

She enjoys spending her time with her husband, David, their son, Grant and their dog, Quinn, and three cats, Kili, Fili and Merlin. Outside of her passion for writing, she loves to cook and bake and trying out new recipes.

For more information on E Whelly and upcoming projects you can visit www.ewhelly.com or check out the following social media pages;

Tiktok: https://tiktok.com/e_whelly

Facebook: https://www.facebook.com/EWhelly

Instagram: https://www.instagram.com/

em_whelly/

Twitter: https://twitter.com/e_whelly

BOOKS BY THIS AUTHOR

The Rise Of Vardya

My Beautiful Ghosts

Mindless Ramblings Of An 18 Year Old Girl: It's Just A Bunch Of Sh*T Poetry

www.ingramcontent.com/pod-product-compliance
Lightning Source LLC
Chambersburg PA
CBHW031635040426
42452CB00007B/847